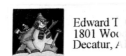

BEAR
BRYANT

CEO

SWEETWATER
PRESS

Bear Bryant, CEO

Copyright © 2006 Sweetwater Press

Produced by Cliff Road Books

ISBN-13: 978-1-58173-584-0
ISBN-10: 1-58173-584-7

Design by Pat Covert and Miles G. Parsons

Printed in The United States of America

BEAR
BRYANT

CEO

Richard Truman

SWEETWATER
PRESS

CONTENTS

THE LOCKER ROOM AND
THE BOARD ROOM

I remember sunny fall Saturdays filled with anticipation of an afternoon game featuring the University of Alabama's Crimson Tide playing under the direction of Paul "Bear" Bryant. I have experienced firsthand the wave of excitement that spread as Coach Bryant followed his players onto the field, and then assumed his famous pose by the goalpost. Victory always seemed to be a sure thing. Whatever problems the team encountered, Coach Bryant would know how to fix them. An overwhelming number of times, he did. I feel privileged to have witnessed his wins and even his losses.

Those legendary Saturdays didn't happen by accident. They were orchestrated and willed by the master of hard work and determination. Though some questioned his methods at times, no one disputed that they worked.

Getting the job done made Bear Bryant's name a household word, and brought him accolades from people from all walks of life.

Fans still mourn the loss of the Bear, but the principles he talked and walked live on. And they are not the worse for wear. Instead, they grow stronger at a time when we're tempted to think that the emphasis is on shortcuts and quick fixes. People are looking for something to believe in that works.

Coach Bryant taught his lessons in the locker room and on the field, but they are just as appropriate in the board room and in the corporate arena. They speak of motivation, determination, hard work, strategy, and most of all, winning. But they include important softer values, too, like loyalty, manners, friendship, and family.

Bear Bryant, CEO offers a collection of Bear Bryant's winning philosophies and attitudes that can be applied to business. Presented in examples from his life, comments of others about him, and from his own quotes, the book will give you a glimpse of his emphasis on excellence in every aspect of his life and how it can be applied to win the corporate game, no matter what level of the business ladder you're on.

Richard Truman

LAYING A FOUNDATION

"He meant every word he said, and he started right on the first day with discipline. He was tough, but I always thought he was fair. He was one of the most organized and dedicated men I've ever been around, and knowing him is one of the best things that ever happened to me."

Jim Blevins

As Coach Bryant established himself and his team at the University of Kentucky, he had the team bused to an isolated military academy twenty-five miles away, where they practiced three times a day. The regime wasn't for the faint of heart. Of the 132 who began, only 40 returned with the team at the end.

Some boys escaped as though they were convicts grasping at their last chance at freedom. As Howard Schnellenberger recalled, "At night, we'd be lying in bed, and you could hear the sound of guys sliding down drainpipes from our two-story dormitory…sliding down so they could escape.…It was a demanding time for all of us. Coach Bryant always made it so difficult that a certain amount would leave, and the ones who stayed had a tremendous amount of commitment to him and the team."

"We can't have two standards, one set for the dedicated young men who want to do something ambitious and one set for those who don't."

Paul "Bear" Bryant

Almost anyone who knows anything about Bear Bryant knows the story of how he took his Texas A&M Aggies for training at Junction, Texas. Following their grueling ten days there, during which many players defected, the team was reduced to just a fraction of its original number. Bryant was approached early in the season about his list of fewer than thirty players. When asked, "You mean this is all the players you got?" Bryant replied, "These are the ones that want to play."

"Formations don't win games, players do. You've got to have chicken to make chicken salad. The players' abilities dictate what you do."

Paul "Bear" Bryant

When Paul Bryant assumed the reins at Texas A&M, he set about to make things the way he wanted them. He was constantly contacted by A&M supporters who thought they were essential to the management of the football team—an opinion not shared by the Coach. Some people even thought his trip to Junction, which became well-known for many reasons, was in part an attempt to get outside the reach of those who offered "help."

But Bryant wasted no time in setting the record straight about his perception of the situation. At the first meeting with alumni after taking the A&M job, he spoke plainly about the situation: "Up to now there have been too many chiefs and not enough Indians around here. From now on I'm the chief and you're the Indians. I know how to coach football. You may think you know how, but I know I do, so I don't need your advice."

"We were in the first meeting with Coach Bryant, and he told us that in four years if we believed in his plan and dedicated ourselves to being the best we could be, we would be national champions. He was right."

Billy Neighbors

Just like he'd done at Texas A&M, Coach Bryant had to clear the air when he took on the head coaching job at Alabama. His predecessor, J.B. "Ears" Whitworth, made a habit of meeting with former Tide players each Wednesday for a few friendly games of dominoes. The talk during those games covered such topics as the direction and progress of the football team, including what the coach was doing wrong.

The group expected Coach Bryant to continue the tradition, and stopped by to see him a few days after he arrived at his new office. They told him they were ready to help him get his bearings, and get the team in order.

But they were in for a surprise. Coach Bryant told them he didn't have time to see them, but they could set up an appointment for any legitimate business at five-thirty the next morning. The group was affronted, and left in a huff, satisfying themselves by saying, "Just wait'll that joker starts losing, and then he'll want our help."

"I have come to Alabama for one reason. To build a winning football team. We are going to do two things. We are going to learn to play football and we are going to get up and go to class like our mommas and poppas expect us to. And we are going to win."

Paul "Bear" Bryant

When Coach Bryant met with his team at the University of Alabama for the first time, he made his intentions clear. He was there to win. Fred Sington recalls the important meeting, and the ground rules Bryant laid down. "He told us, 'I'm not worried about whether I'm going to win or lose. I know I'm going to win. I know that. And I'm not worried about my assistant coaches. I know they're winners. And I'm not worried about whether Alabama is going to win. I know that. The only thing I don't know is how many of you in this room are winners, and how many of you will be with us.' Then he said when he got back we were going to work—and that those of us who were winners would be around to see the rewards, and those of us who weren't, wouldn't."

"Those first few years at Alabama were tough, no doubt about that. It was hard work and it was conducted in one way—the Paul Bryant way. Anybody who didn't buy into his plan had to go."

Jim Goostree

Staffing was another area in which Coach Bryant established himself. When he began his job at Alabama, he made it clear that none of the coaches from Coach Whitworth's staff would be kept on. That left trainer Jim Goostree uncertain about his future. So he asked Bryant, "Well Coach, don't we need to visit?"

Bryant asked him to his office for the discussion. Goostree recalls that "The minute we walked in, he wheeled around and sat me down on the corner of this conference table, and looked me right in the eye, sitting down, he towered over me somewhat. He said, 'I know more about you than you know about me, and if you want to...if you like me, and I like you, after spring practice, you've got a job at Alabama as long as you want one.'"

Goostree responded, "Well, I've got 50 percent of that whipped already. I had better get out of here and go to work on the other half."

CLARIFYING GOALS

Knowing that he was not assistant material was a lesson that Bryant learned the hard way. Restless in his first coaching job as the lowest ranking assistant on Alabama's staff, Bryant accepted an assistant coach's position at Vanderbilt. There, he developed game plans, supervised discipline, and helped evaluate and recruit new players. He took charge of the team for a week in 1940 when Coach Red Sanders collapsed with appendicitis, leading the Commodores to a 7-7 tie with Kentucky.

Sanders fired Bryant at the end of the 1941 season, and many observers say it was because the assistant overshadowed the coach. But a valuable lesson had been learned that helped define Bryant's path toward leadership.

"I tell young players who want to be coaches, who think they can put up with all the headaches and heartaches, can you live without it? If you can't live without it, don't get in it."

Paul "Bear" Bryant

Bryant was a believer in asking for what you wanted, even if you thought it was beyond your reach.

Such was the case when he approached his future wife, Mary Harmon Black, for their first date. Bryant was a football star at Alabama, which gave him entrance into sorority row, but his background hardly placed him on equal footing with daughters of the well-to-do.

But you wouldn't have known it by his approach to Mary Harmon. Running into the beauty at the University's supply store on a fall day in 1934, Bryant worked up the courage to ask her for a date. She took out her appointment book, thumbed through it, and finally suggested a date several weeks later.

Bryant responded curtly, "Shoot, honey; I'm talking about tonight," before he abruptly walked away.

Later that day, he received a call on the community telephone in the gym where he and his teammates lived. It seemed that Mary Harmon had rearranged her calendar, and would be available that night, after all.

"I don't try to save the world. I just go at it one football player at a time."

Paul "Bear" Bryant

Nor was the classic story about how Paul Bryant negotiated a date with Mary Harmon the end of his getting what he wanted. Their dating continued, and it was obvious to all the girls in the sorority house that the two were headed for a walk down the aisle. Indeed, eight months after their meeting on the quad, they were secretly married by a justice of the peace in Ozark, Alabama. Mary Harmon's parents found out about the marriage when they read the announcement in the paper.

The newlyweds kept their marriage a secret because Coach Frank Thomas forbade his players to marry while they were in school. Bryant feared losing his scholarship, so they kept their secret until his senior year.

Bryant took on a wife without knowing how he would support her, much less keep her in the style to which she had become accustomed as she grew up in a well-to-do family. He had thought about becoming a coach, but had no offers. Still, faced with supporting a wife, and soon, a child, he told his roommate, Young Boozer, "Boozer, I'm gonna try to coach. I don't know where, but I'm gonna try to get a job coaching. How 'bout giving me your playbook? Mine's not worth a damn, the way I keep things, but I know you've kept everything Coach's given us in yours. Would you mind? You don't need it anymore, but I could sure use it."

So Boozer, whose plan was to pursue a job in banking back home in Dothan, Alabama, pulled his playbook from his trunk, and handed it to Paul. And so the first steps toward an unparalleled coaching career were taken.

"Don't look back, don't lose your guts, and teach your team to go out on the field and make things happen."

Paul "Bear" Bryant

During Bryant's tenure at Maryland, the school president, Dr. Curly Byrd, insisted that Bryant reinstate a player he had taken off the team for drinking in a bar. The player had connections at high levels of the university.

Bryant considered what he had been told to do, then told the president the next morning that he was resigning instead. A newspaper reporter overheard their exchange, and suddenly the entire campus knew the coach was leaving, and why.

Students were outraged. They threatened to boycott classes, and there was talk of riots, until Bryant addressed the students and urged them to reconsider.

"I could've won that battle," Bryant said. "But I was stubborn and I was going to make my point. The whole thing was based on the fact I would've lost my entire team if I had taken back that player who didn't have the discipline I preached about. Then it came down to me backing down, telling Curly Byrd I wanted to keep my job at Maryland. I wasn't going to do that because I knew I wouldn't be able to look at my face in the mirror." Fortuitously, Bryant returned to his office and found a telegram from University of Kentucky President Dr. Herman Donovan inviting him to lead the program there.

"We're gonna butt heads until I see what I want."

Paul "Bear" Bryant

As the University of Alabama began to deal with Coach Bryant about coming back home as head coach, he was torn between the love that he and his wife had developed for College Station and the desire to Coach at his alma mater. One dominant concern was that he had learned the value of having complete control of the athletic program, and refused to take the job unless he reported directly to the president. He was prepared and eager to be coach and athletic director.

Coach Hank Crisp, who had helped shape Bryant's evolution as a player and a much sought after coach, remained as the athletic director. And it was understood that he would remain in that position when the new coach was chosen.

Bryant faced a dilemma: he was unwilling to accept the coaching job without also having the authority of the athletic director's position. And yet he could not imagine

Coach Crisp remaining and reporting to him. He said that "giving him an order would be like giving his father an order, and he just couldn't do that."

Finally, a compromise was suggested. Crisp agreed to take a job as director of intramurals. But Bryant was not satisfied to get word of the arrangement from the committee. He wanted to hear it from Crisp himself to be sure that he understood the arrangement correctly, and that it really was acceptable to all concerned. He refused to sign the contract until Coach Crisp was agreeable to the change. They met the next day, and Crisp assured him, "I don't care about being no athletic director or no assistant coach. Now, come on. Get your ass back to Tuscaloosa so we can start winnin' some football games."

"When we're not in the running for number one, people know I haven't done my job."

Paul "Bear" Bryant

MANAGING PEOPLE

"The idea of molding men means a lot to me."

Paul "Bear" Bryant

Bryant knew that players could not all be handled the same way. Different players needed different motivation. He always said, "You can't treat them all equally, but you can treat them fairly." And he had more to say about what it took to manage his players and bring out the drive to win: "You have to learn what makes this or that Sammy run. For one it's a pat on the back, for another it's eating him out, for still another it's a fatherly talk, or something else. You're a fool if you think as I did as a young coach, that you can treat them all alike."

"I'm just a simple plow hand from Arkansas, but I have learned over the years how to hold a team together. How to lift some men up, how to calm others down, until finally they've got one heartbeat, together, a team."

Paul "Bear" Bryant

Coach Bryant knew how to get people to play above their expectations. As William Poling said, "Coach Bryant knew more about you than you knew about yourself; he knew when to give you hell, and he knew when to pat you on the back."

"He can take his'n' and beat you'rn—or he can take you'rn and beat his'n'."

Jake Gaither

Bryant's players didn't all love him, but they all respected him. Some wanted to do their best just to please him. Some wanted to do their best to prove that he couldn't run them off. Either way, Bryant produced winners. "He had this incredible ability to manipulate how you felt about him to his advantage," said Harry Bonk, one of Bryant's players at the University of Maryland.

"I don't hire anybody not brighter than I am. If they're not smarter than me, I don't need them."

Paul "Bear" Bryant

"One of his philosophies was he could coach the average athlete and make him better and get 100 percent out of him. I think that is the true trademark of Paul Bryant."

Scooter Dyess

A former team manager under Bryant at Alabama, Gary White, noted that "Coach Bryant had an uncanny knack for reading people—knowing what made each person tick—and when to pat them on the back or kick them in the rump." That was true not only in Bryant's dealings with his players, but with his coaches as well.

An example is the time Clem Gryska, recruiting coordinator, expressed a desire "to be more of the team, you know, contribute a little more to what we're doing in games." Coach Bryant looked at him and said, "Clem, you're a hell of a recruiter. I can go to Birmingham and find a few dozen coaches who can handle the Xs and Os. There are thousands of them across the country who can do that. But there aren't many people who can recruit winning football players."

Gryska went to his office feeling "a dozen feet tall."

"I've been awfully lucky over the years to be surrounded with great people. I don't know if I ever did much for them, but they sure as heck have done a lot for me. When people ask me what

do I want to be remembered for, I have an answer: I want the people to remember me as a winner 'cause I ain't never been nothing but a winner."

Paul "Bear" Bryant

"There's another thing I will always respect about him. When you leave professional football, they send you your pictures in the mail, and that's the last time you ever hear from those people. But Coach Bryant always welcomed us back, and matter of fact, he called me one time when I was playing professional football and asked me how come I hadn't written him a letter!

Another thing he did was when you went to a restaurant or some place with him and people mobbed him. You know most people would get uncomfortable with that or get bothered by that. He never did. He'd get little children and set them in his lap and talk to them, and he'd sign autographs and pictures. He'd sit there and sit there for an hour and do that."

Billy Neighbors

Most Alabama fans will recall the Alabama-TCU game at Legion Field in Birmingham, Alabama, in 1974. They may not remember the score, or even fantastic plays, but they will never forget the injury of TCU player Kent Waldrep that occurred when the junior running back got caught in a rush of players and fell backwards. He was carried out of the game paralyzed by a broken neck.

After the game, Coach Bryant went immediately to the hospital to be with Waldrep's family, and made numerous visits there. As Jack Rutledge, former Bryant player and colleague observed, "Coach Bryant was always positive when he was in the room…Kent said that Coach Bryant and the University of Alabama did more for him than his own school did." Bryant continued to stay in touch even after the family returned home, making frequent phone calls to the Waldrep home until his death in 1983.

But the Bear is continuing to reach out to Waldrep's family in a way even he couldn't have foreseen by way of a scholarship fund he established a year before Waldrep's injury occurred. The fund had originally been set up for any student in need, but was later designated specifically for children of former Tide players after Pat Trammell died.

Now, in an unexpected twist of fate, Waldrep's son is coming to the University of Alabama and will receive a scholarship from the fund due to his unusual connection to the University. His initial visit to campus was followed by an application to the school. When officials learned that he'd be coming their way, they made arrangements for him to receive a scholarship. In a way, the Bear continues to help those who love the game as much as he did.

"I was an athlete, and athletes are driven by motivation and inspiration. And you have to remember that I wasn't that good of a player, and our team didn't have that good of a record. Yet here was the greatest coach ever calling and asking about me. And they weren't just quick calls either. Some would last 30 minutes or more."

Kent Waldrep

MAXIMIZING OPPORTUNITIES

"Most big games are won on five to seven critical plays. The team that makes the big plays wins the game. Lay it on the line on every play. You never know which play is the big play. Try to win on this play. When you get 11 people trying to win on every play, you'll win."

Paul "Bear" Bryant

Growing up on the wrong side of the tracks, Bryant was not the type of young man for whom great things were predicted. Classmate Ike Murray said, "If I had been writing the class prophecy for our senior class, I'd have written this about Paul: 'He'll be lucky to stay out of the penitentiary.'"

But Bryant knew that he wanted to better himself. As it turned out, he discovered football, and made that his vehicle for creating a better life than the one he was given. What he lacked in skill, he made up for in tenacity. His teammate Jack Benham called him "the most aggressive player I ever saw." Bryant played with everything he had because he knew it was his way out. "I hung on as though it were life and death, and it was."

"If you believe in yourself and have dedication and pride—and never quit, you'll be a winner. The price of victory is high but so are the rewards."

Paul "Bear" Bryant

One week after Pearl Harbor, Bryant enlisted in the Navy and said goodbye to his family. It cost him the head coach's position at the University of Arkansas, which was as good as his, but that sacrifice would be repaid when Bryant returned to the sidelines.

When Bryant was assigned to the naval preflight

training school, he incorporated football as a logical component of the training program. Play in many college programs had been suspended because of the lack of players, and military teams formed of former college and professional players became forces to be reckoned with.

Bryant used his influence to have available trainees assigned to North Carolina. Within months, a talented team began to emerge. When it was time for Bryant to return to college football, he had three coaching offers in hand.

"If you're ahead, play like you're behind...and if you're behind, play like you're ahead."

Paul "Bear" Bryant

There are some things that most people can't do anything about. The weather is one of those things. But in the 1976 Liberty Bowl in which the Crimson Tide met UCLA in Memphis, Tennessee, Coach Bryant came face to face with a chance to make the most of an opportunity despite adverse conditions. His critical decision made the difference in ensuring a decisive win for his team.

The game was scheduled on what turned out to be a cold day for the South. The wind was blowing hard, and the wind chill was below zero. And that wasn't the only negative Alabama faced. Bryant's team was 8-3 for the regular season, and they now faced a strong UCLA team.

During the pregame warm-ups, Coach Bryant had his players go out on the field in short sleeved shirts. His intention was to let everyone see how tough his players were in contrast to the UCLA players, who were bundled up, and wearing hoods and gloves. They couldn't catch the ball, their hands were so cold, while the Tide players were running around, acting like it was a normal winter night.

Both teams faced identical conditions. But Bryant's team won because under his leadership, they made the most of the opportunity.

"I'm thankful he grabbed me by the back of the shirt, yanked me up, shoved me back, got my shoulders straight, and refused to let me throw away a great opportunity."

Kenny Stabler

ACCEPTING A CHALLENGE

"What matters is not the size of the dog in the fight, but the size of the fight in the dog."

Paul "Bear" Bryant

Taking on a difficult assignment may have been a common occurrence for the coach, but it was by no means something that he only exhibited as an adult. Growing up on a farm in Fordyce, Arkansas, the young Paul Bryant often walked to town. On one such visit, he saw a poster at the movie theater offering a dollar a minute to anyone who would wrestle a bear. That looked pretty good to a young man chopping cotton for 50 cents a day.

Bryant was able to get hold of the bear securely enough to wrestle him to the mat. He held the bear down, letting the time pass and the money pile up. Bryant recalled, "The man kept whispering, 'Let him up; let him up.' Hell, for a dollar a minute, I wanted to hold him 'til he died." Finally, the bear wriggled out of the muzzle—with possibly a little help from its owner—and bit the young boy on his neck.

Bryant fled, but returned to collect his money. The bear, the promoter, and the money were gone. "I went to get my money after things settled down inside the Lyric Theater and the bear owner had skipped town," Bryant recalled. "All I got out of it was a nickname."

"His nickname was Bear. Now imagine a guy that can carry the nickname Bear."

Joe Namath

Bryant's tenure as head football coach at Kentucky saw him lead the team to win its first conference football championship in 1950. He carried the Wildcats to four bowl games, and won three of those. He was chosen the state's citizen of the year for 1950 as well as SEC Coach of the Year.

Despite those accomplishments, Kentucky was a basketball school and state, and Bryant was forced to take second billing to Kentucky's basketball coach, Adolph Rupp. Bryant finally made up his mind to leave, and accepted the job at Texas A&M.

College Station, Texas, did not offer the Bryant family the social life to which it had been accustomed. But no place could have offered a warmer reception. Bryant was met by several thousand uniformed cadets upon his arrival at College Station. Bryant won their loyalty immediately by walking to the microphone to address them for the first time as their coach. But words were not enough for the new leader of the Aggies. He took off his coat and tie, threw them on the ground, and stomped them. Then he rolled up his sleeves, and said he was ready to go to work. And he did. By the time he left, he had turned the program around, and had produced eleven all-conference players, four All-Americans, and a Heisman Trophy winner.

"Set goals—high goals for you and your organization. When your organization has a goal to shoot for, you create teamwork, people working for a common good."

Paul "Bear" Bryant

Perhaps one of the biggest undertakings of his life occurred in the early seventies, when it became apparent that Coach Bryant might be able to break Amos Alonzo Stagg's all-time NCAA Division 1-A career win record of 314, an amazing record that he had set over fifty-eight years of coaching. Bryant's pursuit of the record began to attract national attention, and only one man, Glenn "Pop" Warner, stood in his way, with 313 wins.

Bryant seemed confident about his chances once he finally admitted his interest in the milestone. "All I know is I don't want to stop coaching and I don't want to stop winning, so we're gonna break the record unless I die. As long as somebody has to be the winningest coach, heck, it might as well be me."

"His last year he was a very sick man, and he willed himself to live—that's exactly what he did. What was driving him to stay alive was to complete the season, to get things in order. I don't know if he himself knew how short his time was, but I think he had the drive and will to complete that season and to have things in order before he died."

Linda Knowles

MOTIVATION

Paul Bryant grew up peddling vegetables off a wagon. He was one of a dozen children, and with his father a semi-invalid, he and his siblings were forced to make ends meet the best ways they could. Even when those days were far behind him, Paul never got past the memory of it. But he used the memory of his humble beginning to motivate him to do his best.

He was often asked about what made him work so hard. "I didn't want to have to go back behind that plow…or peddling through Fordyce with my mama….I was motivated by the fear of having to go back to that more than anything else."

*"Coach Bryant surrounded himself with winning people.
Everyone in the athletic department was part of his family and
contributed to the wins on Saturday—the assistant coaches, the
office workers, the equipment managers, custodians, everyone.
He made all of us believe we could win, not only the players but
all of those other people as well."*

Larry "Dude" Hennessey

Coach Bryant later used all kinds of things to motivate
his players. Nothing and no one were exempt, as Lee Roy
Jordan's story from the 1962 Orange Bowl game against
Oklahoma demonstrates. "President Kennedy was at the
game that particular day, and he had visited the
Oklahoma locker room prior to the game. He was pulling
for Oklahoma because Bud Wilkinson was on his staff for
the Physical Fitness Council. Coach Bryant used that as a
motivating factor before the game and again at halftime.
He didn't miss an opportunity to bring out a little extra
emotion of his team. He mentioned several times that
President Kennedy had ignored us and snubbed us and
played favorites with Oklahoma."

Motivation

"One player you have to shake up and get mad, but you'll break another player if you treat him like that, so you try to gentle him along, encourage him."

Paul "Bear" Bryant

Coach Bryant's skill as a motivator was especially important when his team was behind. Such was the case at Legion Field in Birmingham, Alabama, on October 20, 1979, when undefeated Alabama trailed Tennessee 17-7 at the half. Before Major Ogilvie's touchdown, it had been 17-0. Things looked bleak for the Tide.

Yet when the teams retreated to their respective locker rooms to prepare for the second half, Coach Bryant was calm. He even said that Tennessee was "right where we wanted them." He said, "If you come back and win this game, nobody in the nation will question whether you're the best team in the nation. If you win in the second half, I won't have any doubt you have what it takes to win a national championship."

Bryant's team returned to the field to win 27-17.

"Losing doesn't make me want to quit. It makes me want to fight that much harder."

Paul "Bear" Bryant

Coach Bryant often used subtle ways to motivate his players and coaches. When he did his weekly television show to highlight each week's game, he would often offer comments as game highlights were played: "No, no, that's not the way we taught you to tackle," or "I know Jimmy's Mother and Father are proud of the way he improved his schoolwork."

Players and coaches alike watched for the end of the show, when Coach Bryant showed pictures of players who had had exceptionally good games, as well as pictures of the coaches who had played a key role that week. Coaches knew that if their picture wasn't shown, they would have to work harder the next week.

"There's no substitute for guts."

Paul "Bear" Bryant

One example of Coach Bryant motivating his team occurred at a 1965 game between LSU and Alabama. The game was played in Tiger Stadium, a noisy place to play, which could be distracting for any visiting team not used to it.

On top of that, LSU was using its mascot, Mike the Tiger—a real Bengal tiger—to try to intimidate the Alabama players. Mike was paraded around the field in a show of force, and the home crowd went crazy. To make matters worse, LSU put Mike's cage right outside the Alabama locker room, and poked at him to make him growl loud enough for the Alabama players to hear.

When Coach Bryant arrived at the stadium with his players, he took them on their customary stroll around the stadium. Mike greeted them as they entered their dressing room. Coach Bryant made a point to stop by the tiger cage and say, "I don't know why you're so scared of that cat. That thing must be forty years old."

Just like that, Bryant had put the game in proper perspective for his players. Alabama won 31-7.

HAVING A PLAN

"If you want to coach you have three rules to follow to win. One, surround yourself with people who can't live without football. I've had a lot of them. Two, be able to recognize winners. They come in all forms. And, three, have a plan for everything. A plan for practice, a plan for the game. A plan for being ahead, and a plan for being behind 20-0 at half, with your quarterback hurt and the phones dead, with it raining cats and dogs and no rain gear because the equipment man left it at home."

Paul "Bear" Bryant

Clem Gryska, an Alabama assistant coach, was one who could testify to Coach Bryant's intense preparation for game day. As recruiting coordinator, he worked with the kicking team, and was directed by his boss to take precise measurement of the time it took the team to snap the ball on a punt until the punter kicked the football. He had to check the hang time on punts, and how long it took Alabama to make the tackle on a punt.

Bryant was also interested in the weather, even telling Gryska on at least one occasion, "Clem, I'm not a meteorologist, but that wind looks mighty unpredictable today. Stay on top of it. It might be the difference in winning or losing."

"Little things make the difference. Everyone is well prepared in the big things, but only the winners perfect the little things."

Paul "Bear" Bryant

"It's not the will to win, but the will to prepare to win that makes the difference."

Paul "Bear" Bryant

Coach Bryant expected the preparations before a game to be intense and thorough. And he expected them to be done long before game time, not in the last-minute panic just before the game's start.

Gene Stallings, who many people think walks, talks, and acts like his famous mentor, had this brought home by Bryant once when he was working with players near game time. He recalls, "I was running around before the kickoff one day and reminding players of their assignments. He grabbed me and said, 'If you can't coach 'em during the week, you sure as hell can't coach 'em at one o'clock on Saturday.'"

"I learned more football in one year than I did in the previous three years. He made you learn every position. On defensive alignments, he'd call you up and ask what everybody did. We'd have written tests on everything. We went over everything that could happen in a game. You never saw anything in a game that surprised you."

Fred Sington

Whether he was preparing for meetings, practice, or games, Coach Bryant was thorough in making and executing his plans. In meetings, he would discuss plans until he was certain that he was clearly understood. On the field, he taught by describing the techniques and plays he wanted, demonstrating them, and then having the players perform them, never hesitating to say "That's wrong" if something was not done as it was intended.

Bryant and his coaches covered the basics, even if they were things the players had been doing for years. Butch Frank had this to say about the process: "Here they were teaching 20-year-old players who had been playing football since they were 8 or 10, how to put your hands down in a stance…how to put your toes. How to make your first step, how to make your second step. The minutest detail for every lineman of every technique, it just fascinated me…Nothing was done without a reason."

"We'd better do our homework. And homework means winning."

Paul "Bear" Bryant

Bryant's plans for game day included conditioning his players so they were able to play an entire game and remain fresh. He wanted "somebody who after an hour of playing football would say, 'I'm warmed up now, let's go.'" Bryant's plans paid off. In the 1958 season, for example, Alabama went three games in the middle of the season without calling a single time out. The other teams' players might be tired, but not the Bear's. Gary O'Steen recalls, "You'd just sit there and laugh at them. Really, you just felt so good, you were dancing around over there, these old boys sucking wind, we'd say, 'Oh boy, we've got you now.' That was one of the best feelings in the world."

"I also want my players and coaches and all my staff to learn to have a plan—have a plan in your life and be able to adjust it. Have a plan when you wake up, what you're going to do with your day. Just don't go lollygagging through any day of your life. I hope I have had some luck in my life because I have planned for the good times and the bad ones."

Paul "Bear" Bryant

Coach Bryant thought no detail in preparing for a game was too small to warrant attention. Take, for example, his players' eating habits prior to a game. Especially the games that would lead to his 315th win.

During the fall that would culminate in that historic game, players were put through two-a-day drills. But Bryant was tipped off by the kitchen workers that despite the extra activity, his players were skipping breakfast. Knowing that the boys would not perform well on empty stomachs, Bryant took matters into his own hands.

Mickey Herskowitz offers Warren Lyles' account of what happened next. "Most of us were just too tired to get up so we slept in. One morning one of the guys heard a funny knock at his door at seven-thirty. He shouted and didn't get an answer. He heard the knock again and he got out of bed and threw open the door so he could unload on whoever was there. But it was Coach Bryant. He just said, 'Son, have you been to breakfast this morning?' He said, 'No, sir, but I'm on my way right now.'"

Then Coach Bryant made his way down the hall, continuing to knock on doors and send players to breakfast. Lyles concluded by saying, "None of us missed breakfast after that."

Having a Plan

"Coach Bryant was a stickler for having a plan and sticking with it. He had a plan for every possible game situation; he had a plan for a halftime talk for every possible situation, whether his team was ahead, tied, or behind, and he had a post-game talk for every situation, too, to get the team ready to move on to the next game. He was always prepared, and he had his teams prepared, for any situation."

Lee Roy Jordan

WANTING TO WIN

"If wanting to win is a fault, as some of my critics seem to insist, then I plead guilty. I like to win. I know no other way. It's in my blood."

Paul "Bear" Bryant

Bear Bryant felt a real kinship with Pat Trammell, starting quarterback for Alabama's 1961 national championship team. Bryant called him "the favorite person of my entire life." Their relationship was unlike any other in Bryant's life. As Bryant said, "He can't run well but he scores touchdowns. He doesn't pass well but he completes them. He doesn't do anything well except win." When told of Trammell's death in 1968, Bryant responded, "This is the saddest day of my life."

"If there is one thing that has helped me as a coach, it's my ability to recognize winners, or good people who can become winners by paying the price."

Paul "Bear" Bryant

"One of the first questions he asked me was, 'Do you think you're good enough to make this team?' I'll never forget, I told him I was going to try. He came right back to me and said, 'Let's get something straight right off the bat. We either are or we are not. We're not going to have any triers.' Naturally I told him I was going to make the team. That's the kind of attitude he instilled in us from the beginning. If you didn't think you were good enough, you might as well leave. He didn't want anybody just trying."

Scooter Dyess

"I don't want ordinary people. I want people who are willing to sacrifice and do without a lot of those things ordinary students get to do. That's what it takes to win."

Paul "Bear" Bryant

Despite the number of illustrations that could be given of how Bryant's desire to win manifested itself, no scenario matches his own words on the subject. Here are a few of his classic quotes on being a winner.

"When you're number one, you don't play for the tie."

"The price of victory is high, but so are the rewards."

"My favorite play is the one where the player pitches the ball back to the official after scoring a touchdown."

"My attitude has always been if it's worth playing, it's worth paying the price to win."

"Be aware of 'yes' men. Generally, they are losers. Surround yourself with winners. Never forget— people win."

"I think the most important thing of all for any team is a winning attitude. The coaches must have it. The players must have it. The student body must have it. If you have dedicated players who believe in themselves, you don't need a lot of talent."

REMEMBERING BASIC VALUES

"Many times over and over I heard Coach Bryant preach about playing hard within the rules. In fact, part of that standard talk he made year after year was how he wasn't the least bit interested in hurting another player. He simply wanted us to pursue the football, hit hard, gang tackle, and so forth."

Gene Stallings

Ida Bryant didn't have a lot of material riches to pass onto her children, but she did give them a decent upbringing that included a solid system of values. She insisted on good manners, and her teaching can be seen throughout her famous son's life.

Though the Bear's language could be crude at times, he was always a gentleman in public, especially around women. He never forgot the lessons his mother taught. One episode revolved around his famous hounds-tooth hat, which he was often seen wearing.

In 1975 when Alabama played Penn State in the New Orleans Superdome, the first Sugar Bowl played indoors, Penn State Coach Joe Paterno asked Bryant why he wasn't wearing his trademark hat. He replied simply, "My mama always told me to take off my hat inside."

"I don't make a lot of rules for my players. I expect them to act like gentlemen, have good table manners, be punctual, be prayerful. I expect them to be up on their studies, and I don't expect them to be mooning around the campus holding hands with girls all the time. That comes later, when they're winners."

Paul "Bear" Bryant

When Coach Bryant let his followers at Texas A&M know he was leaving for Alabama, he said it this way:

"Gentlemen, I've heard Mama calling, and now I'm going home."

"One thing that used to impress me about Coach Bryant was that he always returned his calls. It was unbelievable. I was in his office one day, and some woman had called him and wanted to borrow some money from him. He didn't know who she was, but he returned her call. And I've been doing it ever since—that taught me to do it."

Billy Neighbors

Tardiness was to Coach Bryant a sign of lack of commitment and discipline. Whenever he called a team meeting, he made a point to arrive early and then compare his watch with those of others in the room. "What time do you have?" he'd ask. "And you?" When he had responses from all those present, he'd set his watch to the slowest one there. Then when the meeting time arrived, as indicated by his recently-set watch, he would begin the meeting promptly on time. Players learned better than to enter a meeting that was already in progress.

Just ask those who had walked into the first team meeting Bryant held after coming to Alabama. Two minutes into his opening speech, four latecomers tiptoed into the room. Looking straight at them, he screamed, "Get out! Get out!" Then, turning to his coaches, he asked, "Will you have somebody lock the doors? There'll be no interruptions."

Fred Sington was at that meeting and recalls that after the doors were locked, one of Bryant's "best players" tried to get in, couldn't, and started pounding on the doors to get in. Coach Bryant turned to one of his assistants and said, "Go see who that is. And tell him, whoever it is, that we don't need him."

"He was a real gentleman to me and my mother and father. I knew I wanted an opportunity to play for the Tide."

John Mitchell

"I don't want my players to be like any other students. I want special people."

Paul "Bear" Bryant

Coach Bryant learned a valuable lesson on the importance of keeping his word during a trip to visit a player he had heard about. He told the story of stopping in for lunch at "an old cinder block building with a small sign out front that simply said 'Restaurant'" as he recruited in South Alabama during his first year as head coach at Alabama. After he served his already well-known visitor a meal of chitlin's, collared greens, black eyed peas, and cornbread, the owner asked for an autographed picture of the Coach. Bryant took the man's name and promised to send him one later, which he did. It was signed "Thanks for the best lunch I've ever had, Paul Bear Bryant."

Bryant had long forgotten about the incident until many years down the road when he was trying to recruit a young man from that same area. The player originally rejected Bryant's offer, but later called to accept. It seemed that the restaurant owner from years earlier was the grandfather of the young man Bryant was trying to sign.

The boy explained that "you kept your word to him, and to Grandpa, that's everything." Bryant recalled the incident by saying, "I was floored. But I learned that the lessons my mama taught me were always right. It don't cost nuthin' to be nice. It don't cost nuthin' to do the right thing most of the time, and it costs a lot to lose your good name by breakin' your word to someone....I made it clear to all my assistants to keep this story and these lessons in mind when they're out on the road. And if you remember anything else from me, remember this: It really doesn't cost anything to be nice, and the rewards can be unimaginable."

"You don't win on tradition; you win on blocking and tackling on the field. But I do think tradition is important in that it gives the players and coaches something to live up to."

Paul "Bear" Bryant

When Coach Bryant presented a weekly television show to review each week's game, he was told that his show was only the second-rated sports show in the nation. When he asked, "Who in the hell beat us?" he was told that the *Bart Starr Show* in Green Bay was first. "Well that's okay, Bart's one of ours," he replied.

Among all the eulogies and remembrances that were offered in the days following Coach Bryant's death, Steadman Shealy recalled a scene in the Alabama locker room immediately following the 1982 Liberty Bowl. "I was a couple of people over from him, on my knees, and he was on his knees. Here was the greatest coach of all time, and he wasn't too proud to get on his knees before God. He said, 'Lord, thank you for allowing me to be a part of football, to be a part of this team, to be a part of this university, and for these many happy years in coaching.'"

"Coach Bryant was a very compassionate and caring man. He did a lot of things for people that are not known. We had an old janitor in what we call the 'old building' from back in the early sixties, and his name was Hooch Man. He was an elderly, black gentleman, and Coach Bryant gave him a room in part of our office building to live in, bought him a TV, and gave him a monthly check out of his personal bank account for his expenses. Coach Bryant looked after him until he died."

Linda Knowles

Writer Al Browning recalls a conversation in Coach Bryant's office in which the topic turned to the Coach's retrospective view of his life. He expressed the thought that "I should've taken the time to get to know a lot of good people a whole lot better." Browning assured him that perhaps other people might be at least partly to blame for not reaching out to him, thinking he was above the need for fellowship with others. Bryant replied, "Maybe so, at least in some cases. But I'm the one who should've reached out. Remember, Alfred, you've got to treat other people the way you want to be treated."

"You can learn a lot on the football field that isn't taught in the home, church, or classroom. I'm a pretty good example of that."

Paul "Bear" Bryant

Some readers will remember that Coach Bryant made a television commercial for South Central Bell late in his coaching career. The script was written to end with his saying, "Have you called your mother today?" When he taped the commercial, his true feelings came out when he ad libbed the line, "I sure wish I could call mine."

With that line, he had expressed his heartfelt emotion about his beloved mother. The producer at first thought the line would ruin the commercial, but when production was finished, and the commercial began to run on television, everyone agreed that the unplanned sentiment had literally made the commercial. According to Coach Bryant's wife, he received letters not just from every state in the union, but from all over the world.

The footnote to the story should not be surprising either. Coach Bryant did not keep any of the money he earned from the commercial. Instead, he used it to set up a college education fund to help students who couldn't pay for their education.

UNDERSTANDING LEADERSHIP

"But it's still a coach's game. Make no mistake. You start at the top. If you don't have a good one at the top, you don't have a cut dog's chance. If you do, the rest falls into place. You have to have good assistants, and a lot of things, but first you have to have the chairman of the board."

Paul "Bear" Bryant

One of the first steps in being a leader is to realize that you cannot settle for anything less than being the leader...not even the most prestigious assistant's job will do. Paul Bryant knew he was not cut out to be second chair. And others knew it too. Early in Bryant's career, he applied for an opening on Frank Howard's staff at Clemson. Howard could see that Bryant would not be able to work for someone else. Years later, he summarized the situation by saying, "There was no way I was about to hire Bear. In no time, he'd have slit my throat, drank my blood, and had my job."

"Leaders say let's go, not sic 'em."

Paul "Bear" Bryant

Some leaders expect those who work for them to be "yes men," rubber stamping decisions without daring to disagree. But according to long-time associate Charley Thornton, that was not the case with Coach Bryant.

As he recounts in *The Legend of Bear Bryant*, Thornton met with Bryant to discuss a public relations job. When Bryant told him to go upstairs and check out the publicity office, Thornton offered his evaluation that "Coach, it's terrible." Equipment was old, in some cases rusted, and outdated. Thornton told him what was lacking, and that what they did have was just too old. The Coach responded with, "Well, you can buy equipment, can't you?" sealing the deal with Thornton, who would handle Bryant's publicity, and later be his assistant athletic director, for the next twenty years.

Thornton summed it up this way: "It didn't take long after I went down to Alabama, to recognize that most of the people there were more afraid of Coach Bryant than I was. Maybe I didn't have real good sense and should have been. Don't get me wrong. I was as intimidated by him at times as anyone else. But I think he trusted me because when I didn't think something was right, in my area, at least, or if he asked a direct question, I told him what I thought. He kind of liked that."

"I don't think it would have mattered what occupation Coach Bryant had chosen. He was a pure leader, a take charge person. I'm sure he would have been a masterful military officer. At the same time, he would have been just as skillful as the chairman of the board for a huge corporation. It just so happened that football was his business, and I don't think anybody would doubt he elevated himself to the top of the ladder in that sport."

Jim Goostree

Coach Bryant held his players to rigorous standards, even when it was a talented player, and even when it cost the team as well as the individual. Joe Namath was a case in point.

Namath arrived at Alabama with plenty of talent, but his behavior off the field caused him problems. At the end of a 10-1 season during his sophomore year, Namath and friends visited a local bar, had drinks, then wrecked a car on their way back to school.

Bryant personally visited Namath in the athletics dorm to ask about the incident, which Namath admitted. Bryant called a staff meeting to decide Namath's fate. Most of the coaches believed it should be overlooked. Gene Stallings said, "If it had been me, you would've fired me." Bryant agreed, saying, "Then I think that's what ought to be done."

Bryant suspended Namath from the team for the remaining regular season games, and a Sugar Bowl game. He explained, "If you were allowed to stay on this team then I would have to resign, because I'd be breaking my own rules." He told Namath he could return once he got his personal life straightened out. Steve Sloan stepped in for the two games Namath missed, but Namath returned the following year and led the Crimson Tide to a national championship.

Namath later credited Bryant for his own success, stating, "He was there for me when I needed discipline. He picked me up and shoved me forward when I needed to be kicked in the butt."

"You could walk into a meeting room, and you could hear yourself breathe. You could hear your own heartbeat. Everyone had so much respect for Coach Bryant."

Jim Bunch

Pre-game meals were special times for Coach Bryant's players. Observers said that players leaned forward to hear the half-growled speech of the Coach.

Bryant usually invited other faculty members to attend, hoping to emphasize the integral relationship of all parts of the University. At one meeting, the guest was the dean of the English department, who later said, "If I could get my students in the palms of my hands like Coach Bryant can, I would teach for the rest of my life for nothing."

"Coach Bryant inspired such awe and respect. I remember one time we had a reporter in from one of the major newspapers—it seems like it was the New York Times—who I'm sure had interviewed kings and presidents and whatever. That man went into Coach Bryant's office and never sat down throughout the whole interview. He was that awed by Coach Bryant's presence, and he made a comment about it when he came out of the office. He said, 'I've handled a lot of things, but this is pretty awesome.'"

Linda Knowles

Gene Stallings recalls coming face to face with the tremendous respect that even game officials had for Coach Bryant.

It happened in the 1967 Cotton Bowl, when Stallings's Aggies were playing Bryant's Alabama team. In a third-down situation, Coach Bryant mistakenly thought it was fourth down, so he sent his punter in. In response, Stallings sent in a safety who could only field punts.

Bryant's coaching staff quickly let him know about the

mistake, so he sent in another player and the punter came out without playing, even though rules at that time said that when a player went into a game, he had to play one down. Likewise, Stallings sent in an appropriate player, and asked the safety to come out. Officials were quick to let him know his player had to stay in for a one play. Stallings responded, "Now, wait a minute, fellow. I'm sitting right here watching Coach Bryant send his punter in, and then Coach Bryant took his punter out!"

The official summarized the whole situation by simply saying, "You ain't Coach Bryant!"

"This must be what God looks like. He'd walk into the room and you wanted to stand up and applaud."

George Blanda

"I have been fortunate enough to know some of the most powerful individuals in the world, but none matched Paul in charisma and talent. He was the best leader I ever knew."

Aruns Callery

George Lapides, who began his sports reporting career in Memphis, was fortunate to have developed a personal relationship with the legendary Coach. Lapides recalls, "I was very young and hardly knew anyone outside of Memphis when I became sports editor of the *Memphis Press-Scimitar*. When I went out of town to cover events such as SEC meetings, I'm sure I looked lost and intimidated, because I was. Bryant sort of took me under his wing and made sure I met everyone he thought I needed to know. I've always thought he felt sorry for me."

Charley Thornton, Alabama's sports information director under Bryant, offers this point of view: "There were a select group of writers that Coach Bryant especially trusted and George was one of them. He always made sure that those writers got good stories from him."

"I don't know what he had, but he had a lot of it."

Bobby Marks

One characteristic that many people appreciated in Coach Bryant was that no matter how many records he set, and no matter how many important people he knew, he never got too big to do the ordinary jobs. One sportswriter tells of being in Bryant's office one day when the phone rang. Bryant excused himself, and picked up the receiver. Then he said, "All right, just let me get a pencil. OK, Dozen eggs. Carton of milk. Loaf of bread…" It soon became apparent that he was taking down a grocery list from his wife.

GIVING IT ALL YOU'VE GOT

"You'd better know something about work, discipline, and sacrifice in life. You'll need it."

Paul "Bear" Bryant

As a child, Bryant had endured ridicule from his classmates because of his humble lifestyle. Though he is often said to have been from Fordyce, writers who referred to that town were often corrected as Bryant emphasized that his real hometown was Moro Bottom, though it wasn't a real town at all.

There was always a group of "city" boys and girls waiting to tease poorer children like Bryant. He always felt inferior when he heard their taunts, and never forgot how they stung. "I can pass that school now and hear those voices....I still remember the ones that did it."

Bryant used the sting of that time to fuel his desire to succeed. He needed to prove to himself, and to those that thought they were better than he, that he could be something. He turned their jeers into cheers. As his sister Louise later said, "He was never ashamed of where he came from or having been poor, but he never forgot the ones who belittled him and our mother. He was determined to show them he was made of something special."

Though he was more aggressive than coordinated as a student athlete at the University of Alabama, Bryant tackled every job with enthusiasm and determination. Such was the case when he attempted to pitch in a team baseball outing.

Focused on the job at hand, he drew back and threw the ball as hard as he could. Unfortunately, it landed on catcher Charlie Marr's forehead instead of in his glove. Witnesses said you could have read Spalding on the site of impact. Marr was knocked unconscious, and remained out until the trainer brought him to with smelling salts.

Bryant's efforts may have been misdirected, but no one could say he didn't approach his assignment with everything he had.

"I'm no smarter than anybody else, but I may work a little harder."

Paul "Bear" Bryant

A sign that hung in the locker room of the University of Kentucky while Coach Bryant was there simply said, "Be good or be gone."

"I've never seen a person work so hard in my life. Coach Bryant demanded the same thing from all of us."

Steve Meilinger

Paul Bryant was a believer in making the most of every situation. He realized the value of living every moment to the fullest. His feelings about this were particularly well expressed by a short poem that he often shared with others titled "What Have I Traded." He professed to have read the poem daily as inspiration to make the most of each day, and kept a copy on his desk.

This is the beginning of a new day.
God has given me this day to use as I will.
I can waste it or I can use it for good.

What I do today is very important because
I'm exchanging a day of my life for it.
When tomorrow comes this day will be gone, forever,
Leaving something in its place I have traded for it.

I want it to be gain, not loss, good, not evil,
Success, not failure, in order that I shall not
*   forget the price I paid for it.*

"Paul Bryant prepared his team physically and mentally and expected 110 percent effort from everyone on his staff. He remembered those who laid it on the line for him. When I was asked why I stayed at Alabama, I have two reasons. I didn't like to lose and I knew we weren't going to lose very often, and I didn't have enough nerve to tell Coach Bryant that I was leaving for another job."

Jim Goostree

"I'm not much of a golfer, I don't have any friends, and all I like to do is go home and be alone, and not worry about ways not to lose."

Paul "Bear" Bryant

Bryant once said, "I'd probably croak in a week if I ever quit coaching." Ironically, he died thirty-seven days after coaching his last game.

"There's a lot of blood, sweat, and guts between dreams and success."

Paul "Bear" Bryant

Coach Bryant was said to have a plaque in his home that read, "Ask God to bless your work. Do not ask Him to do it for you."

"I had a health checkup. The doctor said everybody ought to take a day off and do nothing. That'd drive me crazy."

Paul "Bear" Bryant

TEAMWORK

"One man doesn't make a team. It takes 11."

Paul "Bear" Bryant

When Bryant took his Texas A&M team for the controversial training at Junction, one of the players that went with him was Fred Broussard, who had earned All-Southwest Conference acclaim the previous year. Bryant, however, felt he could do more, and was determined to get the player to do his best. He saw Broussard as one of the most talented players on the team, but felt that his performance so far fell short of what he was capable of. So he pushed Broussard hard.

One afternoon following a scrimmage, Broussard

threw his helmet down and walked off the field. Bryant called out to him, "Now, Fred, if you don't come back you'll regret it the rest of your life." But Broussard kept walking.

The next day, the player had a change of heart and wanted to return. Other players even intervened on his behalf, but Coach Bryant was adamant that Broussard had made his decision. There was nothing to discuss. As the Coach explained to reporters, "He wanted to come back. He told me he had thought it over and that he was sorry, but I told him mine wasn't a hasty decision, either. I told him 'no' because I thought it was best for the team."

When asked what the press should be told, given Broussard's all-conference status, Bryant replied, "Just say Broussard quit. Q-U-I-T. That's all."

Not allowing Broussard to return had not been a decision Bryant made lightly. He was certainly needed. The season was two weeks away, and now the team had lost one of its best players. As Keith Dunnavant has summarized, "A lesser coach might have taken him back, maybe punished him in some way, but Bryant would not let the big picture be obscured by short-term needs. It wasn't the first time Broussard had quit and begged for forgiveness; he had done so two or three times with the previous coach, Ray George. As much as he wanted to win immediately, as badly as he needed an experienced center to snap the ball in the Aggies' season opener, Bryant realized that taking Broussard back at that particular moment would have conveyed the wrong message about discipline and commitment to his football team."

"People who are in it for their own good are individualists. They don't share the same heartbeat that makes a team so great. A great unit, whether it be football or any organization, shares the same heartbeat."

Paul "Bear" Bryant

At the conclusion of the 1982 season, Coach Bryant announced he was retiring. He said he had made the decision because he wasn't pleased with himself anymore. "This is my school, my alma mater. I love it and I love my players. But in my opinion they deserved better coaching than they have been getting from me this year."

"I think one of the great things he did was to get individuals to sacrifice their own egos for the good of the team. He'd get them so centered on one goal that they were willing to literally lay their lives on the line."

Sylvester Croom

"I told them my system was based on the 'ant plan,' that I'd gotten the idea watching a colony of ants in Africa during the war. A whole bunch of ants working toward a common goal."

Paul "Bear" Bryant

"If everyone pulls together, and if everybody puts his best foot forward, we can have a real fine football team."

Paul "Bear" Bryant

Teamwork was not just for the players. It was the concept that Bryant sought to instill in his coaches as well. Although Bryant was ultimately in charge, each coach had an assignment and was expected to contribute in his area. As the one in charge, Bryant took blame when coaches and players alike failed to perform up to expectations.

Clem Gryska, Alabama's recruiting coordinator under Bryant, found Bryant's willingness to take the blame the most impressive aspect working with the Coach. "You never heard him criticize a player. You never heard him criticize an assistant coach. You always heard him say something like, 'I just didn't do a good job telling the offense what to do in a certain situation,' or 'I just didn't have our defense prepared for this or that.'" Even at staff meetings, he would speak for the group, saying, "We didn't do a good job."

"Winning is a 'we' thing, not a 'me' thing."

Paul "Bear" Bryant

"In order to have a winner, the team must have a feeling of unity; every player must put the team first—ahead of personal glory."

Paul "Bear" Bryant

DOING THE IMPOSSIBLE

"You never know how a horse will pull until you hook him to a heavy load."

Paul "Bear" Bryant

John David Crow, one of Bryant's Texas A&M players, recalled that "Coach had this uncanny ability to make you believe that no matter how bad the situation was, you could do whatever you had to do to win."

An incredible example was the Texas A&M game with Jess Neely's Rice Owls in 1955. Things didn't go at all in favor of A&M, and, with only two minutes left to play, Coach Bryant's team trailed 12-0. But even after Rice had just apparently sealed the deal with a final touchdown, Bryant gathered his starters and reminded them, "There's still time, men. You can still win, if you believe you can."

A couple of critical substitutions later, and things turned around. Time was running out, but soon the score was 12-7. Then, after Gene Stallings recovered an onside kick near midfield, Jimmy Wright threw the ball to Lloyd Taylor who caught it, scored, and kicked his own extra point.

But Bryant's team wasn't finished. Intercepting a pass made by a desperate Rice team, Jack Pardee set up the final touchdown by Don Watson. In the space of just over two minutes, the Aggies had salvaged the game, and won 20-12.

"He did a magnificent job and just about the impossible. A&M is better off for his having been here. We certainly wish him well."

A&M President Dr. Chris Groneman

Doing the Impossible

Just before Alabama's game against Auburn in 1961, the team realized there was a problem with its shoes. Something about the way the grass was cut made getting secure footing difficult.

Coach Bryant placed a call to former Crimson Tider Fred Sington, who owned a chain of sporting goods stores all over the state, asking him to find as many pairs of a certain type of shoe as he could for the team. Then Coach Bryant made a special effort to have the shoes delivered to his team, calling on the State Troopers' Office to arrange an escort for the shoes as they were rushed to the team in time for the game.

The next morning, players from critical positions reported to the parking lot, where they found all those shoes. Billy Richardson describes the result of the Coach's unusual effort: "We ran through some plays in the parking lot and everybody agreed those were great shoes. They were ideal for what we had in mind for the game. We got a big victory that afternoon, 34-0, and I remember those Auburn players looking at those shoes with expressions on their faces that said, 'Oh no, it looks like you've gone one up on us again.'"

"Americans have lost a hero who always seemed larger than life, a coach who made legends out of ordinary people. He was a hard, but loved, taskmaster. He was patriotic to the core, devoted to his players, and he was inspired by a winning spirit that would not quit. 'Bear' Bryant gave his country the gift of life unsurpassed. In making the impossible seem easy he lived what we strive to be."

Ronald Reagan

Many fans and players alike thought Coach Bryant had supernatural connections. If they thought he could walk on water, they found out for sure that he could control the weather when the team was invited to play in the Sugar Bowl in New Orleans at the end of the 1963 season. Tim Davis recalls, "I remember someone saying that Coach had been to a meeting before the Sugar Bowl, and said, 'We've got about as much chance of winning down here as it has of snowing.' I woke up the day before the game and looked out the window [and] saw snow outside our hotel window! And I'm saying, gee whiz, this is amazing, snow falling down in New Orleans."

The Tide defeated Ole Miss 12-7.

OVERCOMING OBSTACLES

"He always stressed to all of us that we had to fight, and he didn't mean fistfighting. He meant when things were their bleakest, to suck it up and make something positive happen, and you could overcome the worst adversity."

Dude Hennessey

During Bryant's senior year as an Alabama student, 1935, he broke the fibula in his right leg during a loss to Mississippi State. He spent the next week on crutches, never expecting to play in the upcoming Alabama-Tennessee game. But he dressed for the game, planning to watch from the sidelines.

In an emotional pre-game locker room speech, Coach

Crisp looked each player in the eye as he spoke. "I'll tell you gentlemen one thing," he said as he paced. "I don't know about the rest of you...but I know one damn thing. Old 34 will be after 'em, he'll be after their asses."

Bryant couldn't believe his ears. The coach was talking about him. Rising to the challenge, Bryant played in the game, having what some considered to have been the game of his career. He scored on a long touchdown pass, lateraled to Riley Smith on another scoring play, and made major defensive stops to help Alabama defeat Tennessee 25-0.

One reporter was so taken with Bryant's performance, he asked to see x-rays to convince him that Bryant really had a broken fibula. Fans showed their appreciation at the next game by giving Bryant a standing ovation for his courage. "That's the only one I ever got as a player," he said. But of the experience, Bryant said, "It hurt like hell, but it was just one little bone."

"Coming from behind is still one of the greatest lessons, and the ability to do it is the mark of a great team."

Paul "Bear" Bryant

Jim Bunch, a former player of Bryant's, tells of a time when he was able to overcome an injury and play well, thanks to Coach Bryant's expectations. It was his junior year, and the Crimson Tide was facing Florida. Bunch wasn't supposed to play because of an ankle injury. The coach came by before the game and asked how he felt. Not realizing that Bryant was asking if he was fit to play, Bunch replied, "I'm great, Coach."

Bunch was put in at right tackle. "I wasn't even supposed to play. All of a sudden, that pain in my right ankle disappeared. The adrenaline rush of knowing that I was going to play…it was probably the best game of my junior year."

"In a crisis, don't hide behind anything or anybody. They're going to find you anyway."

Paul "Bear" Bryant

One of the most upsetting episodes in Coach Bryant's life occurred when he and Georgia's Coach Wallace Butts were accused of fixing the outcome of a game between their teams.

The game was played on September 22, 1962, in Birmingham, Alabama, and Alabama won 35-0. The *Saturday Evening Post* published an article claiming that Butts had told Bryant via telephone the strategy the Bulldogs would use. The information was supposedly exchanged to allow the two coaches to place bets on the outcome. And there were allegations that other games had been fixed.

Bryant was alerted to the article before its publication, thanks to an advance copy provided by friends. He conferred with university officials, then told his players about the furor to come. Armed with the truth, verified by his passing a polygraph test about the allegations, Bryant faced a television audience on his regular *Bear Bryant Show*.

Looking directly into the camera, he told the people of Alabama up front that he was not guilty of fixing a ballgame. John Forney, longtime play-by-play voice of Alabama football, was in the studio to witness the statements by Bryant. "Coach Bryant had many crowning moments during his years at Alabama. However, I'm not sure he was ever any better than he was on television that Sunday afternoon. All he did was tell the truth."

"It's an old story. You stick your head above the crowd, and you're going to have people try to knock your block off."

Paul "Bear" Bryant

GIVING CREDIT

"*When you win, there's glory enough for everybody. When you lose, there's glory for none.*"

Paul "Bear" Bryant

In response to praise that came his way, Bryant responded, "I am, I think, just an ordinary coach that works hard. Some work a little harder than others. But it's players who make the coaches, my friend. And the mothers and papas have a lot to do with making players, too."

"*I don't have any ideas; my coaches have them. I just pass the ideas on and referee the arguments.*"

Paul "Bear" Bryant

Who can forget Alabama's outstanding defensive effort during the 1981 Alabama-Penn State game as Bryant was closing in on his famous 315th win? The Tide held against a powerful Penn State team throughout the game, but was especially effective during the third-quarter when they kept the Lions from scoring on seven straight plays inside the Alabama seven-yard-line. The Tide won 31-16 to give Bryant his 314th win, and a tie with Alonzo Stagg as the winningest coach of all time.

Bryant acknowledged the effort in a gesture intended just for those involved. Tommy Wilcox recalls, "As the defensive team came off the field after those seven plays, there was Coach Bryant, three or four yards out on the field. He took off his hat and tipped it to us as we came off as if to say, 'Job well done.' When he took his hat off to us, I had goose bumps all over. At that moment, I felt bigger than a mountain."

"I've never won a game. I've been blessed with good players who were winners."

Paul "Bear" Bryant

When efforts were underway to build a Bryant museum on the campus of the University of Alabama, Bryant enlisted the help of Al Browning to help organize the work. But he insisted, "I don't want a damn shrine built for me. But some people want to build something, so I've agreed as long as it's a shrine built in honor of all of my former players, assistant coaches, and a lot of other people at Alabama, Texas A&M, Kentucky, and Maryland. It's going to be like that or we aren't going to do it."

Bryant was as adamant about accepting responsibility when something went wrong as he was about giving credit when things went well. "If we have an intercepted pass, I threw it. I'm the head coach. If we get a punt blocked, I caused it. A bad practice, a bad game, it's up to the head coach to assume his responsibility....If anything goes bad, I did it. If anything goes semi-good, we did it. If anything goes really good, then you did it."

PERSEVERANCE

"There is a big difference between wanting to and willing to."
Paul "Bear" Bryant

Bryant always wanted to know where he stood with his players—who was dependable, and most importantly, who was not. "If a man's a quitter, I want him to quit in practice, not in a game." He expected "all they've got. We've got to know now whether we can get it later."

"The first time you quit, it's hard. The second time, it gets easier. The third time, you don't even have to think about it."
Paul "Bear" Bryant

Despite his continual urgings to never give up, Bryant knew how players felt when they considered that option. When he started his academic career at Alabama, he was lonely and homesick. And he felt inferior because of his country background. After he received word of his father's death, he wrote his cousin that he was considering leaving and getting an oil job.

His cousin immediately replied in a telegram: "Go ahead and quit just like everybody predicted you would." Bryant's jaw was set after that. He later admitted staying because "I wasn't about to quit after that."

As a coach, he remembered how it felt to stand at that crossroad, and often gave his players the same choice— making a commitment of all their abilities, or returning home a quitter.

"But there's one thing about quitters you have to guard against —they are contagious. If one boy goes, the chances are he'll take somebody with him, and you don't want that. So when they would start acting that way, I used to pack them up and get them out, or embarrass them, or do something to turn them around."

Paul "Bear" Bryant

"Never quit. It is the easiest cop-out in the world. Set a goal and don't quit until you attain it. When you do attain it, set another goal, and don't quit until you reach it. Never quit."

Paul "Bear" Bryant

"I'll never give up on a player regardless of his ability as long as he never gives up on himself. In time he will develop."

Paul "Bear" Bryant

"There was one thing I always remember about playing for the University of Alabama: We had an inner strength, a tenacity, an arrogance that we would find a way to win. We really didn't talk about such things, but Coach Bryant instilled this factor into us. A lot of teams we played against, even though they may have been ahead of us and had better players than us, well they really weren't sure if they could beat us. There were a lot of teams that played us tooth and nail in the first half, and in the second half we'd wipe them out."

Byron Braggs

LEARNING FROM MISTAKES

It should be no surprise that Coach Bryant recruited new players with the same enthusiasm that he did everything else. One dragnet for new players was particularly notable in that the Coach learned a lesson he would not forget, or repeat.

As he began his work at Texas A&M in the fall of 1954, Bryant and his staff made the rounds to recruit new players. They had a large freshman class to help flesh out scrimmages, but who could not compete in varsity games. Freshmen would remain ineligible for varsity games until 1972.

To help the coaches' efforts, several well-intentioned Aggie boosters made illicit inducements to young men considering playing for A&M. Bryant privately approved their actions. The following spring, two of the young men signed affidavits stating that they had been paid a small amount each, and had been given the promise of extra money per month above their scholarship to attend A&M. The Conference and the NCAA moved quickly to place the Aggies on two years' probation, which would also preclude the Aggies from bowl appearances for two years, and would invalidate more than one hundred letters of intent.

Bryant paid a surprise visit to the NCAA's infractions committee, which was charged with doling out punishment in such cases. After discussing particulars of the case he asked, "You mean to tell me that an alumnus can't give these kids money?" He was told by committee Chairman Ab Kirwan, "Of course he can't, Paul. He can't do that." Bryant responded with, "Well, I guess I don't have anything to argue about."

More than a decade later, Bryant admitted, "I know now that we should have been put on probation....I'm not sure how many of our boys got something. I guess about four or five did. I don't know what they got, and I didn't want to know, but they got something because they had other offers and I told my alumni to meet the competition." His candor was stunning. The admission left him with a sense of failure, but he vowed that it would not happen again, and, indeed, it never did.

"When you make a mistake, admit it; learn from it and don't repeat it."

Paul "Bear" Bryant

Vito "Babe" Parilli was one of Bryant's best players during his tenure at Kentucky. And yet Bryant almost overlooked this player that he would later call "the best fake-and-throw passer I have ever seen."

As a single-wing halfback in high school, Parilli was recruited by dozens of major schools. The year before Parilli graduated, he visited Lexington with a friend, a much sought-after running back who later signed with Ohio State. Bryant saw the two boys during their visit, but was not impressed and did not follow up with Parilli.

However, in his senior year, Parilli became such an extraordinary passer that he was courted by many coaches, including Bryant. When Bryant visited in Parilli's home, he invited him to visit the Kentucky campus, and was surprised when Parilli responded, "Coach, I've already seen it, I was there with a friend last year." Bryant recalled that he had indeed seen the young man before. Realizing that his oversight almost lost Parilli before he had a chance to woo him, Bryant asked for another chance and promised Parilli a different reception next time.

Parilli later said, "Coach Bryant sure kept his word about that. When it came time to sign, he sent Carney Leslie to pick me up in a limousine. He told me we were going to Pittsburgh, to Forbes Field." They went, however, straight to Lexington. According to Parilli, "We were on the road, fifteen or sixteen hours, maybe more. But while we were on the road, there was no chance of any other school getting to us. I think they called it kidnapping back then."

"Coach Bryant never made excuses for losing, and more than anybody I've ever seen, he tried to benefit from each loss."
Paul "Bear" Bryant

One of the most publicized of Bryant's training methods was the rigorous training camp he held for his team in Junction, Texas, in the late summer of 1954. When they returned, the number of players had dwindled from over a hundred to a mere twenty-seven. Players disappeared in the night, unable to meet the seemingly impossible demands Bryant placed on them. Although insult was added to injury when the team returned home from the brutal training to suffer through a 1-9 season, the team always ranked among Bryant's favorites for all it endured.

Bryant was asked about the experience many times during his life, to which he responded that he had done the only thing he had known how to do. He was firm that he would not do it again "because I know more now than I knew then—more about resting players, letting them drink water, more about other ways to lead them…I believe if I had been one of those players, I'd have quit, too."

"I've had a full life in one respect, but I've had a one-track deal in another respect. My life has been so tied up with football it has flown by. I wish it wasn't that way, but it has gone by mighty fast. Practice, recruiting, and games; there hasn't been anything except football."

Paul "Bear" Bryant

Even when Bryant was not able to correct a mistake, he was able to learn something that would make him a better coach. Such was the case as he dealt with Kenneth Hall at Texas A&M.

Every college in the country wanted Hall. As a high school senior in Sugar Land, Texas, he had rushed for more than four thousand yards and scored a state record of fifty-seven touchdowns. The Aggies signed him even before Bear became the coach there.

By the time he was a senior, Hall was playing with greater frequency, and became a starter when fullback Jack Pardee was sidelined with a leg injury. With four games remaining, and number one ranking in the team's pocket, Bryant believed the combination of Hall and John David Crow would be unstoppable.

But on Monday before the Arkansas game, Hall failed to show up for practice. Bryant assumed he had quit the team. When Bryant arrived home that night, Hall met him on the front steps, and begged for another chance. Bryant agreed. However, Hall failed to show up again the next day. He met the Coach at his home again that night and again, begged for another chance. But Bryant reluctantly dismissed him.

Bryant blamed himself afterward for mishandling the young man, believing in retrospect that he had needed guidance instead of harshness. We can only assume that the incident and what he learned from it helped him reach out to other players in need later.

"When you get beat, no one can be satisfied, and around me they'd better not be satisfied."

Paul "Bear" Bryant

BREAKING NEW GROUND

"Football changes and so do people. The successful coach is the one who sets the trend, not the one who follows it."

Paul "Bear" Bryant

Coach Bryant was an innovator in many ways. One was his simple creativity in teaching his players new plays. An example was the chair drill he put together when the team went to the 1959 Liberty Bowl in Philadelphia.

Billy Richardson describes the drill this way: "We had 11 chairs lined up in the offensive position and 11 in the defensive position, just plain old folding chairs. We sat down in the chairs, and Trammell would call a play and the snap, then we would point at whatever direction or chair you were going to. It was a mental drill. Well the next day we got the headlines in the Philadelphia papers. None of those guys had ever seen anything like Coach Bryant's chair drills."

"Paul Bryant is changing the way football will be played in the Southeastern Conference from this day forward with Alabama's helmet-busting, gang-tackling style of defense."
Ralph "Shug" Jordan

One of Bryant's most significant achievements was to lead the University of Alabama in freeing itself from the bonds of racial prejudice. When he began coaching at his alma mater, the school and the football team were both entirely white.

Even when Coach Bryant was at the University of Kentucky, he went to his president, Dr. Herman Donovan, telling him "he could be the Branch Rickey of the Southeastern Conference if he allowed Bryant to integrate his football team." But Donovan declined, and another decade would pass before real progress was made.

Stories say that Bryant's mind was opened to the value of black players after Sam "Bam" Cunningham led Southern Cal to defeat Alabama 42-31 in 1970. After the game, Bryant invited Cunningham, a Mobile native, into the Tide locker room and said, "This is Sam Cunningham. This is what a football player looks like."

Alabama signed its first black recruits that year. John Mitchell, a Mobile native, became the first black athlete to play for Alabama when he started defensively against Southern Cal in Los Angeles in September 1971. Wilbur Jackson, from Ozark, Alabama, had been the school's first black signee.

"In 1959 Coach Bryant brought his Alabama team to Philadelphia to play Penn State in the first Liberty Bowl. Not many leaders in the South had the courage to leave the South and play an opponent, much less one with a black player. He always wanted Alabama to be more than a regional team, and I think that is what separated him from his peers in his conference and why Alabama was a team with a national reputation."

Joe Paterno

At the end of the 1960s, Bryant's Crimson Tide suffered a slump in its performance, with 6-5 and 6-5-1 records in 1969 and 1970, respectively. In addition to just barely making the bowl list, it missed the AP top twenty lists both of those years for the first time since 1958.

As an alumnus of Alabama, and as its current football coach, Bryant was unhappy with the performance. It didn't take him long to assess and correct the situation. He made no secret that "I'm through tiptoeing around and I'm through pussyfooting around. I'm going back to being Paul Bryant and anybody who doesn't like the way Paul Bryant does things can get the heck out of here."

Noting that friend Darrell Royal's Texas Longhorns had won national championships the last two years with a new formation called the wishbone, Bryant decided to employ it himself. The style proved to be a perfect fit for Bryant, his coaches, and his team.

Bryant studied his notes, looked at films, and spent the entire summer planning the change. Just four days before fall practice began, he announced to his staff that they were going to install the wishbone. And there was no wavering or turning back. "We're going to sink or swim with the Texas stuff" he said. "This isn't a trial, it's a commitment."

If the change was not radical enough in itself, the timing made it so. Most major changes are usually made in spring training, not mere weeks before an opening game. But all the assignments were changed and preparations were made with only weeks to perfect the details.

Bryant revealed his new strategy at Alabama's meeting with Southern Cal in the fall of 1971. Somehow, he had managed to keep the whole thing a secret until the opening kickoff. Southern Cal was obviously taken off guard, and Alabama pulled off a surprising 17-10 upset over a team that had humiliated the Crimson Tide the year before. Making the victory extra sweet was that it gave Bryant his 200th career victory.

Bryant's willingness to begin something new paid off in a big way—it brought Alabama back to the national spotlight.

"Paul Bryant was never inflexible when it came to changing with the times, and that's just one of the marvelous traits that separated him from the ordinary. He was a liberal thinker when it came to football and the motivation of people, and when he told me in 1971 that he was determined to move

Alabama back to its accustomed slot in college football, I never doubted he would do it."

Alf Van Hoose

It wasn't just in strategy that Bryant was willing to change. He was willing to reconsider his position on smaller details of his players as well. For example, students in the 1970s began to wear longer hair. Bryant had always insisted his players keep their hair short, but even he came to realize that he needed to give a little about this.

After giving it some thought, Bryant called his friend Derrell Royal and said that he'd noticed while watching a recent game that Texas players were wearing their hair longer. Royal acknowledged that the times had changed, and he was changing with them. Besides, he said, "I can't see that another inch or two of hair makes much difference." He had only to point to his team's 30-game winning streak as proof.

Following the conversation, Bryant called in Johnny Musso to ask him again, "Why in God's name do you want hair hanging out of your helmet? Musso replied simply, "It's important to us."

Bryant made what seemed to him a big concession by saying, "If it's important to you—and damned if I know why—then go ahead and let it grow. But keep it clean."

"My football players have changed, and as a result I've changed. I don't pretend otherwise. For example, I let them wear their hair longer now. I don't mean they go around looking like sheepdogs, but by my bowl-cut standards it's pretty darn long. Used to be I'd have jerked it out by the roots if a kid wore long hair."

Paul "Bear" Bryant

DOING IT RIGHT

"George Bush could walk in the door and it wouldn't bother me because once you've worked for Coach Bryant, you can handle anything."

Linda Knowles

Coach Bryant always believed he was teaching more than football. "I believe there are certain things you can't learn in school, in church, or at home. Football teaches a boy to work and instills him with many of the attributes he needs to compete in life." Marty Lyons echoes this, saying, "I will always remember Coach Brant saying, 'A winner in the game of life is that person who gives of himself so other people can grow.' I think you can take all the awards you win and all the championships you win, and you can put those in the closet compared to what Coach Bryant taught you off the field. I think the one thing Coach Bryant did was make you believe in yourself. He believed in his players, and by having him believe in you, it made you believe you could accomplish anything on and off the football field."

"The things Coach Bryant taught me have followed me through life. They have impacted my marriage and the way I have raised my children."

Lee Roy Jordan

Early in his tenure at Kentucky, Coach Bryant took his team on what he portrayed to be a "retreat, actually a farm near Lexington." Just because they were away from campus didn't mean that rules didn't still apply. One way in particular that the Coach had to enforce regulations was that when a player was late for practice, Coach Bryant would hand him a shovel, and issue instructions for him to go to a nearby cow pasture and shovel cow chips for an hour or so.

On one rare occasion, Bryant overslept and arrived about fifteen minutes late for practice. No one mentioned it at first, but at the end of practice, Pat James stepped up and handed his coach a shovel.

Knowing he was guilty, and accepting the same punishment he doled out, Bryant took the shovel without a word and went to the pasture to begin shoveling.

"I'm a product of the Paul Bryant school of life, the Alabama football program, and I'm proud of that."

Jackie Sherrill

Despite the harshness of the ten days Bryant put his Texas A&M players through at Junction, many mark it as a turning point in their lives. Bobby Drake Keith recalled that "Junction and the experience of playing for Coach Bryant taught us all a tremendous amount about discipline, sacrifice, perseverance, hard work."

Another player, Lloyd Hale, echoed this sentiment. "Coach Bryant taught us to give it everything you've got and to never quit, no matter what. That carries over into so many things."

"The biggest thing when you play for Coach Bryant are [sic] the lessons, the things he said over and over again. When you're that age and he's telling you about discipline, he's telling you about hard work, he's making you work hard, he's talking about cooperation, and having guts and hanging in there when it gets tough. You hear it over and over again, but you really don't understand it.

"Finally, about your junior year, maybe you start to relate it to what's happening on the football field. But you don't really understand until you start making house payments, you get on the job and you lose a job, you get in a situation where you don't know where your next check is coming from, you're having problems with your kids or your wife or things are just going tough in general. That's when you find out what he was really talking about.

"To me, that's what the goal line stand represents. You've got your back against the wall, and you've got two choices: You hang in there tough and get the job done or you quit. Once you

quit, you die. So many times those lessons have come back to me. It's those lessons that you learn while playing for Coach Bryant that you remember when the going gets tough. You always remember, if I did it one time, I can do it again."

Sylvester Croom

Gaylon McCollough is another former player that recalls an important lesson he learned from Coach Bryant.

It was Alabama's 1965 Orange Bowl game against Texas, and Alabama was trailing. Joe Namath had the ball, plunged into the line, and ended up at the bottom of a pile in the end zone, thinking he had made a touchdown. One official thought so too. There was confusion on and off the field about whether Namath had actually scored. The call was contested, and once a decision was reached, officials placed the ball on the 6-inch line, blew the whistle, and announced it was first down, Texas.

Alabama players were stunned, but were forced to return to the game as it continued. One player muttered, "We scored" as he passed by Coach Bryant, to which the Coach responded that if Joe had walked into the end zone with the football, there would have been no question about it. Observers would later see the Coach whisper something to Joe as he trotted off the field following the incident. According to the Bear's own recollection, he told Joe it didn't make any difference. "If you can't jam it in from there without leaving any doubt, you don't deserve to win."

McCullough offered a broader application of the lesson: "If you want to accomplish something in life, don't do just enough to get the job done because the world's referees might not make the correct call, either. If you really want to do something, go beyond what is expected and leave no room for doubt."

"The old lessons (work, self-discipline, sacrifice, teamwork, fighting to achieve) aren't being taught by many people other than football coaches these days. The football coach has a captive audience and can teach these lessons because the communication lines between himself and his players are more wide open than between kids and parents. We better teach these lessons or else the country's future population will be made up of a majority of crooks, drug addicts, or people on relief."

Paul "Bear" Bryant

Laurien Stapp, one of Bryant's players, tells the story of carrying a play in during a game near the end of Bryant's career. Bryant had originally circled one play on his notebook, but had scratched through it, and had chosen another play instead. Stapp didn't realize the change, and carried in the original play, which resulted in a touchdown. But, as Stapp recalled, "Coach Bryant let me have it after that play, even after we had scored. He was really steaming. He put more emphasis on me following instructions than the touchdown."

"Don't do it the easy way, do it the right way."
Paul "Bear" Bryant

The stories surrounding Joe Namath's years as a player under Coach Bryant are too many to count, but one that may have been overlooked in the headlines, from which the famous player drew a life lesson, occurred in his sophomore year.

Namath was playing poorly, and Bryant sent word for him to come out of the game. As he came to the sideline, he threw his helmet to the ground in anger, where it took an unfortunate bounce and landed at the feet of Coach Bryant.

Bryant looked calmly at the helmet as it came to a stop, then went over and just as calmly sat next to Namath on the bench. He even put his arm around him in what seemed to be a fatherly gesture. But according to Namath, Bryant was actually squeezing the back of Namath's neck, while promising him, "Boy, don't ever again let me see you coming out of a ball game like that. Don't ever do it again or you're gone."

Once Namath explained that he was only mad at himself, the Coach replied, "Okay, Joe. I understand."

"I believe a football player who comes here [the University of Alabama] and stays four years is going to be better prepared to take his place in society and better prepared for life because I think he'll learn some lessons that are very difficult to teach in the home, in the church, or in the classroom. I think that by learning these lessons, he'll win."

Paul "Bear" Bryant

SHOWING CLASS

"If we lose, I'll be bleeding on the inside, just like always, but I'll still try to smile on the outside and congratulate the other team and coaches."

Paul "Bear" Bryant

Alabama met Ohio State in the 1978 Sugar Bowl. The game was significant because Alabama was in the running for a national championship, and a win could help in that effort.

During the third quarter, it was announced that Notre Dame, ranked fifth, was beating Texas by a large margin in the Cotton Bowl. That meant it was shaping up to be a competition between Alabama and Notre Dame for the number one spot.

It was obvious that Ohio State was no match for Alabama. Coach Bryant was undecided about whether to run the score up, making Alabama a more obvious choice for number one, or to give all his players a chance to play. He finally decided: "I'm going to play them all."

It was a decision that may have cost him the title he coveted for his team. Though Alabama won the United Press International championship, Notre Dame moved from fifth to first, and won the Associated Press poll. But even in the face of disappointment, Coach Bryant stood by his decision. As Mal Moore recalls, "He told me there wasn't any way he was going to humiliate Woody Hayes, the famous Ohio State coach, and he said it was only right that our down-the-line players got a chance to play in the Sugar Bowl after working as hard as they did during practice all year." Moore continued, "I don't know if you'd term that compassion, but you'd certainly call it a show of class."

"It was definitely something special when Coach Bryant and Coach Woody Hayes coached against each other in the 1978 Sugar Bowl. We won it, 35-6, and it looked a whole lot easier than it really was. Those were two great coaches. It was a

privilege to play under Coach Bryant, and it was a privilege to help win that game for him. Of course, as always, we had a masterful game plan to use against Ohio State."

Major Ogilvie

When Coach Bryant started laying down the rules for his Alabama team, he was clear that he would expect his players to behave like the winners they were. "There's only one thing I expect…When you are out in public you represent this football team and you represent the state of Alabama, and you are to act accordingly. If you don't, you will have to answer to me."

"There's a difference between a football player and an Alabama football player."

Paul "Bear" Bryant

"Show class, have pride, and display character. If you do, winning takes care of itself."

Paul "Bear" Bryant

Coach Bryant demanded that his players act like gentlemen, and that one way they could do this was to conform to a dress code—coats and ties on road trips, and hair neatly cropped. Although he would eventually ease up on his requirements for hair styles, he continued to insist on players wearing ties.

In his last season, Alabama met Penn State in Birmingham. As the players filed in for breakfast, he announced, "Nobody in here is going to eat anything until every player is wearing a tie." Players scrambled to find ties, some even borrowing them from hotel employees and guests. Clem Gryska watched as his wife went to their room, got his ties out of the suitcase, and tossed them down from the second floor into the lobby. Players reached up to grab them as they floated down. Gryska noted, "One of our quarterbacks…couldn't find anything but a big yellow ribbon, which he tied around his neck."

When all players returned dressed to suit the Coach, he announced, "Now y'all look a hell of a lot better, and I think you'll play a lot better because of it."

He must have been right. Alabama beat the Nittany Lions 42-21.

"I always want my players to show class, knock 'em down, pat 'em on the back, and run back to the huddle."

Paul "Bear" Bryant

"When you get in the end zone, act like you've been there before."

Paul "Bear" Bryant

"Don't talk too much. Don't pop off. Don't talk after the game until you cool off."

Paul "Bear" Bryant

"It's awfully important to win with humility. It's also important to lose. I hate to lose worse than anyone, but if you never lose you won't know how to act. If you lose with humility, then you can come back."

Paul "Bear" Bryant

Coach Bryant never thought salary was the most important consideration in his taking on a job. He tried to avoid political problems that might be caused if he accepted a salary that was out of line compared to other professors and department heads. Although he could probably have named and received any salary he wanted, even at Alabama when he was nearing his record-setting

315th win, his salary was said to be well below those of other Southeastern coaches.

Instead, Bryant accepted responsibility for his own financial security, and it was his astute business dealings that made him wealthy. He readily acknowledged that his well-placed connections had been invaluable in business. "A football coach really lives football, but making a living at the same time is difficult. I've been lucky that I've had a lot of good friends who've helped me make money. Some of 'em have helped me make money without me taking a chance of losing money, and that's the kind of friend we all want to have."

"I don't know what class is, but I can tell you when someone has it. You can tell it from a mile away."

Paul "Bear" Bryant

Perhaps nothing he did revealed his own class so much as the way Paul Bryant relinquished his job as head coach at Alabama when he realized he could no longer fulfill its obligations. Although his staff maintained that even in his final season of coaching they saw no lessening of his abilities, he felt it. He could no longer promise new recruits that he would be their coach for four years. And the 1982 season that had started with such promise was soon marred by losses, not the least of which was Alabama's 23-22 loss to Auburn. Even in the midst of that stinging defeat, Bryant was gracious in congratulating his former assistant, Pat Dye: "First of all, I'd like to congratulate Pat and his team. He certainly did a fine job today as he has all year."

Two weeks later, he offered his resignation to a packed news conference at the University. Though Bryant planned to stay on as athletic director for a while, Ray Perkins was announced as his replacement. Some have said that Bryant had submitted a list of people he recommended for consideration, but that his recommendations were not considered. If that was the case, he did not indicate his disappointment. Instead, his parting words spoke eloquently of the goals he had pursued and the love he still felt for his school:

> *There comes a time in every profession when you need to hang it up, and that time has come for me as head football coach at the University of Alabama.*
> *My main purpose as director of athletics and head football coach here has been to field the best possible*

team, to improve each player as a person, and to produce citizens who will be a credit to our modern day society.

We have been successful in most of those areas, but I feel the time is right for a change in our football leadership. We lost two big football games this season that we should have won. And we played in only four or five games like Bryant-coached teams should play. I've done a poor job coaching.

This is my school, my alma mater, and I love it. And I love the players, but in my opinion they deserve better coaching than they've been getting from me this year. My stepping down is an effort to see that they get better coaching from someone else.

It has been a great job for me, personally, to have the opportunity to coach at my alma mater. I know I will miss coaching, but the thing I will miss most is the association I have had with the players, the coaches, the competition—all those things that have made such a strong tradition at Alabama.

BIBLIOGRAPHY

Bolton, Clyde. *The Crimson Tide. A Story of Alabama Football*. Huntsville, AL: The Strode Publishers, 1972.

Browning, Al. *I Remember Paul "Bear" Bryant*. Nashville, TN: Cumberland House Publishing, 2001.

Dunnavant, Keith. *Coach. The Life of Paul "Bear" Bryant*. New York: Simon & Schuster, 1996.

Forney, John, and Steve Townsend. *Talk of the Tide*. Birmingham, AL: Crane Hill Publishers, 1993.

Herskowitz, Mickey. *The Legend of Bear Bryant*. New York: McGraw-Hill Book Company, 1987.

Lapides, George. "The Bear's Last Game." *Memphis Flyer*, December, 1999.

Melick, Ray. "Bear's Gift to a Rival." *The Birmingham News*, June 11, 2006.

Shafer, Jack. "The Tao of Bear." *Slate*. Fri., May 16, 2003.

Stoddard, Tom. *Turnaround*. Montgomery: Black Belt Press, 1996.